BREAKTHROUGH IS IN YOU

CONQUER 5 FEARS THAT KEEP YOU FROM ADVANCING

For foreign and subsidiary rights, contact the author.

Cover design by: Joe De Leon
Author photo by: Andrew van Tilborgh

ISBN: 978-1-954089-40-2   1 2 3 4 5 6 7 8 9 10

Printed in the United States of America

BREAKTHROUGH
IS IN YOU

CONQUER 5 FEARS THAT
KEEP YOU FROM ADVANCING

JEFF SCOTT SMITH

AVAIL

DEDICATION

This book is dedicated to my parents, Wheeler and Ann Smith. Though my father passed away in 1993, his and my mother's love, support, and example continue to inspire me greatly. Through them, I have learned to love God, people, and life.

Their lives are examples of breakthrough. I witnessed the principles in Breakthrough Is in You *through them firsthand over the years. The treasures that my parents deposited in me were not only spoken about. They were demonstrated daily, and I hope to pass them on to my family and others for generations to come.*

God blessed me incredibly by giving me the wonderful privilege of being parented by Wheeler and Ann Smith. I am eternally grateful to God and them for loving me into a life of purpose.

Fears are educated into us, and can, if we wish, be educated out.
—Karl Augustus Menninger[1]

---

1   Dr. Karl Menninger, Map of Kansas Literature. Accessed April 15, 2021. https://www.washburn.edu/reference/cks/mapping/menninger/index.html#:~:text=%22Fears%20are%20educated%20into%20us,satisfaction%20usually%20find%20boredom%20instead.%22.

FOREWORD

I am proud to have the opportunity to comment on the first book by Jeff Scott Smith. I am more blessed, however, to have had him by my side for 20 years. Serving in nearly every aspect of local church ministry, I have watched him develop and evolve into a leader to leaders and a consultant to many organizations.

In *Breakthrough Is in You*, he draws upon his experiences and paves a clear biblical path toward advancement. Conquering the five fears he outlines will make you bigger and better at anything you attempt.

I think you will find this book an easy read due to its conversational style. What you can read in one sitting has the potential to change forever where you are standing.

Get busy!

—Bishop Michael S. Pitts,
Senior Pastor, Cornerstone Church Toledo, Ohio

PREFACE

Breakthrough Is in You

*No passion so effectually robs the mind of all its
powers of acting and reasoning as fear.*
—Edmund Burke[2]

Mom, I'm calling to you from the top of the world!"[3]

Thirteen-year-old Jordan Romero spoke these words when
he called his mother, Leigh Ann Drake, from 29,035 feet above
sea level on May 22, 2010. Imagine what was going through
Drake's mind as she watched her son on a GPS—Global Posi-
tioning System—tracker as he became the youngest climber to
reach the summit of the tallest mountain in the world, Mt. Everest.
Certainly, there were lots of tears and declarations of "I love you!"

---

2 Terror. Burke, Edmund. 1909-14. *On the Sublime and Beautiful. The Harvard
Classics.* Accessed December 21, 2010. http://www.bartleby.com/24/2/202.html.

3 Blanc, Katherine, and Jordan Romero. *The Boy Who Conquered Everest: the Jordan
Romero Story.* Bloomington, IN: Balboa Press, 2010.

But just think of the multitude of emotions both of them must have felt during such an exciting and record-breaking event.

As a leader pondering this story, several questions came to my mind. *What is it that would cause Jordan Romero to think about climbing the tallest mountain in the world? What would inspire him to dream that big? What would motivate him to go through all the training required to prepare his body for climbing a mountain of that height? Why would he subject himself to all those dangers? Is it the desire to be great, to break a record, or just to climb a mountain because it is there?*

It made me think, then, of other breakthrough people: Roger Bannister, who was the first to break the 4-minute mile; Henry Ford, who revolutionized the automobile industry; Neil Armstrong, who walked where no man had ever walked before; and Rosa Parks, who became a catalyst for the civil rights movement.

What do all these people and those who are going to accomplish remarkable feats have in common? It is a dynamic called *breakthrough*. Breakthrough energizes people to dare to do what others say cannot be done. It occurred to me that every one of us is a potential breakthrough person. If that is so, why do so few of us ever actualize or live out that potential?

I believe that the answer is simple: fear. This book will introduce you to five fears that you must conquer to be a breakthrough

leader who inspires others to break through. At the end of each chapter, I have provided strategic questions that you can use to engage your mind to begin thinking triumphant thoughts. Join me as we embark on this exciting journey to breakthrough.

ACKNOWLEDGMENTS

It has been my experience that while on this journey we call life, the significant moments and accomplishments in my life have all been the result of relationships that I hold dear to my heart. As I complete this book, I am reminded of the tremendous gift with which God blessed me —my parents, Wheeler and Ann Smith. I pray the rich deposit they placed in me will be passed down for generations to come.

That deposit continues to be encouraged by the tender yet strong love of my wife, Nicola, daughters Lauren and Kristin, and son, Jeffrey. They are the joy of my life, and I am so proud of each of them.

In addition, I want to express great gratitude to Bishop Michael Pitts, who has not only mentored me but also invested in me for nearly two decades. Without the experience, exposure, and example he has given to me, my life would not be the same.

Having someone who believes in you and encourages you to keep reaching higher is an invaluable gift. Dr. Samuel Chand is such a gift to me.

I am also extremely appreciative of the hours and energy that my assistants, Susie Hieber, Leah Parker, and Dr. Kefa Otiso, have given to this project.

Thanks to God for all these relationships and many more that have shaped my life and helped me continue to break through.

CONTENTS

CHAPTER 1

BREAKTHROUGH IS IN YOU

He has no hope who never had a fear.
—William Cowper[4]

I love being around people who have faith, who have optimism, enthusiasm, and excitement—those who have dreams.

In life, many difficulties will try to stand between you and where you are going, between you and your dream or vision. But if you possess what I like to call this dynamic of breakthrough, you can overcome any obstacle, break through any barrier, and see your dream come to pass, even though it might seem impossible. If you are reading this book, I believe that you can experience breakthrough in your life, and you can lead others to their breakthroughs.

Breakthrough is the capacity, ability, and power to overcome obstacles and break barriers. It is the aptitude to succeed where

---

4   "He Has No Hope Who Never Had a Fear." William Cowper: He has no hope who never had a fear. Accessed December 21, 2010. https://www.quotes.net/quote/12172.

others fail and to overcome obstacles that hinder others. I want to show you how to increase that capacity and ability and venture forth in that power more dynamically in your life, so you can go where you are supposed to go, and others can follow your example. To do that, though, you must believe that you can go farther in life than where you are right now.

To set the stage for this concept of breaking through, I want to share with you the portion of scripture that triggered this notion of breakthrough for me.

> *When the time came for her to give birth, there were twin boys in her womb. As she was giving birth, one of them put out his hand; so the midwife took a scarlet thread and tied it on his wrist, and said, "This one came out first." But when he drew back his hand, his brother came out, and she said, "So this is how you have broken out!" And he was named Perez. Then, his brother, who had the scarlet thread on his wrist, came out. And he was named Zerah.*
> —Genesis 38:27-30 (NKJV)

This portion of scripture is part of an incredible story in Genesis 38. Here, we find a lady named Tamar who is pregnant with twins and about to give birth. Though she conceived in unusual circumstances, she had a strong desire to have a child because she understood the promise that was on the family of Judah. She understood the destiny that was to come to that lineage. Out of Judah's loins, there was

believed to be a line of kings through which the Messiah would ultimately be born. Some say that she so desperately wanted to see this happen and be a part of it that she tricked her way into it. When Judah went back on his word to give her to his son Shelah in marriage (see verses 11 and 14), she refused to take no for an answer and took matters into her own hands. Her tenacity caused her to make a way for herself and apprehend the desire of her heart and forever edge herself into the house of Judah and—ultimately—the lineage of Christ (see Matthew 1:2-3).

I love this story because there is something that always happens around the time of birthing. Anticipation, excitement, and intensity build. When I read this passage, I was reminded of when my wife and I had our first child. I remember being so excited that I could not wait! This was our first child, and we did not know how everything was supposed to happen. I remember that it was a Saturday night, and we had just come home from shopping when my wife announced, "Uh-oh. I feel something moving."

And I replied, "Uh-oh!"

So, we headed to the hospital, thinking that our firstborn was getting ready to arrive on the scene. We got there, and the doctor looked at us and said, "I think you both are just excited. You are not going to have a baby tonight. You guys just go on back home."

We were disappointed because we had thought we were going to have a baby that night. We went home, and I tried my best to calm my wife down by getting her water, massaging her back, rubbing her feet, and so on. Then at two o'clock in the morning, our baby girl decided she was coming! We rushed back to the hospital, and a few hours later, our first child was born. I will never forget what an exciting time that was!

Going back to Tamar, we see that something quite interesting happened at her time of birthing. Remember that she was pregnant with twins, so there were two babies in the womb. The first child was ready to be delivered, but the first body part to came out was a hand instead of the head! Perhaps the midwife did not catch the significance of that because it is not normal. In a normal delivery, the head comes out first. In this case, the hand came out first—which lets us know that something unusual was about to happen.

When the midwife saw the hand, she wrapped a scarlet cord around it and declared, "This one came out first." Then scripture says that the child, the one who should have been first, drew his hand back and, unexpectedly, the second child came out first! They named this child Perez, which means "to break through, to overcome." The midwife then asked this question: "How did you break forth?"

So, how did Perez break forth—break through? This is the question that I would like to address in *Breakthrough Is in You* so that you can learn and apply the principles to achieve breakthrough

in your own life as a leader. Only then will you be able to forge a path for others to follow.

For this book, I am using Zerah to represent Christ and Perez to represent a believer. Zerah was the one who had the opportunity to be born first. Instead, he withdrew his hand and allowed Perez to go. While he had the right to be born first, he willingly came second. In the process, he made a way for Perez to follow. Perez can represent a Christian who maximizes the moment and walks through the opportunity that Christ has made for him and thereby achieves breakthrough.

If you simply believe that God is able—even when situations and circumstances are stacked against you, when the odds seem like you should not come out on top, when the statistics say that a loss is coming our way—He will make a way and give you the ability to come through with the victory in your life. In short, God is for you even if it does not look like it, and He is for those you lead, so His greatest desire is to grow you so that He can grow them. Just as Zerah made a way for Perez, Jesus has already gone before you and made a way. All you have to do is have the courage and faith to walk on that path to breakthrough and victory.

Whatever you are facing, you have to believe that you will come through with the upper hand. Your job situation might look like there is no way you will get promoted, but you have to understand that if God is working on your behalf, it does not matter what

anybody says or what anybody is doing. You will come through with the victory. You have to believe that even if the enemy is fighting you through your children, and it looks like they are not serving God—they are trying to go as far away from Him as they possibly can—you will still come through with the upper hand. You have to believe this even in the realm of your finances. It might look like foreclosure or bankruptcy. It might look like everything is getting ready to fall apart in your situation. Still, if you believe that God is able, if you believe that He has the power to change the situation, to shift your circumstances, He will do so and cause you to come through, seeing His blessing released upon your life. But, once He makes a way for us, it is up to us to apprehend and walk out the victory.

Do you know a promise is waiting for you and those you lead? Are you willing to fight for it for yourself and others? God wants to do something great through you and on your behalf, but He wants to know if you have something on the inside that says, "I will fight to get what He has determined for my life. I refuse to let anything or anybody take what God has for me." Perez had the dynamic called breakthrough in him. It is as if he said, "Since my brother's hand has gone before me and given me a head start, I must seize the moment and get out of this womb first. I need to get out of this place of limitation where I cannot walk, stretch, or move freely."

Some of you might think it is too late, that there is no time for you or yours, or that circumstances are not in your favor, but I want to encourage you that it is not over—for anyone—until it is over. If you keep fighting, if you keep pressing, if you keep pushing, you will come out with the upper hand, you will be the one who gets the blessing, you will be the one who gets the breakthrough, and you will be the one who sees the promises of God become a reality in your life and in the lives of those you lead.

You must believe that the capacity for breakthrough is in you, and it is on us corporately as believers. You are anointed to break through and to overcome. You are anointed to succeed where others have failed, win where others have been defeated, and see harvest where others have experienced famine.

Unfortunately, life has a way of making breakthrough difficult. It has a way of putting you in confined, limited, and restricted places, much like a womb. But, when you have the dynamic of breakthrough working in your life, it gives you the calm, the confidence, and the courage to push back and break free. Be determined not to live your life in a box. Experience the freedom and liberty you were created to enjoy!

It has been said that *fear* stands for False Evidence Appearing Real. Life certainly has a way of presenting you with evidence that is contradictory to your hopes and dreams. It will present you with evidence designed to keep you complacent and compliant with the

limitations and boundaries that keep you from embracing your God-given potential. Life will try to tell you that you are not good enough, smart enough, rich enough, or beautiful enough, and the list goes on. Friend, you must remember that this is nothing more than false evidence, it will produce a fear that will keep you from breaking through barriers and walking in victory.

Fear can come in many different forms and facets. It is no accident that the phrase "Do not be afraid" occurs close to seventy times in the NIV translation of the Bible. If you can deal with these fears and teach your people to do the same, they will no longer hinder you and hold you in the limited places that you may find yourself in currently. You can come up to another level of effectiveness, fulfillment, success, and power. Just like Perez, you can break forth from your womb, your confined space, and step into a world of unlimited potential.

In the following chapters, I want to walk you through five distinct fears that you must overcome to see the dynamic of breakthrough manifest in your life and the lives of others. They are the Fear of the Unknown, the Fear of Failure, the Fear of Going First, the Fear of Investment, and the Fear of Opposition. They are all present in Genesis 38:27-30. Let's take a closer look at each of them.

CHAPTER 2

THE FEAR OF THE UNKNOWN

Do not be afraid to go out on a limb. That's where the fruit is.
—H. Jackson Browne Jr.[5]

*Have no fear of sudden disaster or of the
ruin that overtakes the wicked.*
—Proverbs 3:25 (NIV)

I t was 1961, and the Soviet Union had just launched the first man into space. President Kennedy responded to this extraordinary feat by saying, "I believe that this nation should commit itself to achieving the goal, before this decade is out, of landing a man on the moon and returning him safely to Earth." The race in space was on between two countries who were sworn enemies fighting what would become a decades-long Cold War. From 1963 to 1965, it looked like the Soviets were winning the race as they

---

5 Standfield, Ken. Essay. In *Intangible Risk Management Standards: Introduction*, 166. Service Productivity Pty Ltd., 2006.

launched the first woman, landed the first satellite, and performed the first spacewalk.

The American race into the unknown met with tragedy on January 27, 1967. The crew of the American *Apollo I* were killed in a fire on the launchpad. Later that same year on April 23, tragedy struck again when a Soviet cosmonaut died because his spacecraft's reentry parachute failed. These incidents caused both countries to stop flights for an entire year. However, the Soviets continued working in secret. When NASA resumed its space program, the Soviets had already scheduled their subsequent missions. No one knew what they were planning. Maybe it was to place a man on the moon!

On July 16, 1969, *Apollo 11* was ready for liftoff. Just a few weeks earlier, the Americans had spotted a huge Soviet rocket. Days later, the ruins of this rocket were seen on a satellite. It had blown up. If America could avoid catastrophe, the nation would reach the moon and win the race into the unknown.

Buzz Aldrin, Neil Armstrong, and Michael Collins were the astronauts selected for this history-making mission. All three men spent countless hours in preparation, weeks stretching into months. Armstrong mastered flying the lunar module *Eagle*. Collins perfected eighteen different rendezvous points for the command module *Columbia*. Aldrin perfected simulated moon-walking.

They were preparing for an experience like none before. They were going to walk on the moon.

Final preparations were made. They spent their last weekend with their families. They knew they might not ever return. On July 20, 1969, the crew flew facedown through space, then flipped over and saw Earth one-quarter million miles away. They fired the engines when they were only twelve minutes from landing on the moon. As they approached, the computer onboard became overloaded, lights began to flash in the cockpit, and a "program alarm" sounded off. Armstrong and Aldrin faced the Sea of Tranquility, the place where they were scheduled to land. Shockingly, it was a sea of rocks! Armstrong barely cleared the boulders and flew over the craters. Finally, he saw an open spot to land. He needed to come down perfectly or risk damaging the spacecraft. Astonishingly, they landed safely. Armstrong climbed out of the spacecraft and positioned a television camera. Now over 600 million people could watch as he became the first man to touch the moon's surface. He then spoke his famous words: "That's one small step for man, one giant leap for mankind." [6,7]

Making the journey into the unknown is filled with uncertainty and unexpected events. However, the rewards can be monumental. By breaking the fear of the unknown, you open up possibilities

6   Chaikin, A. A Man on the Moon: The Voyages of the Apollo Astronauts. New York, NY: Penguin Putnam, 1995.

7   French, F. and Burgess, C. In the Shadow of the Moon—A Challenging Journey to Tranquility 1965-1969. Lincoln, NE: University of Nebraska Press, 2007.

to do what you have never done before and to be who you have never been before.

Many people live life wanting all the blanks filled in. They want to see the agenda, the plan, and every step to how everything is going to work. Before they get on board, they want to have everything explained. Before they invest time or energy, they want to have a cup of coffee with you.

But, if you have lived long enough, you know that life does not work like that. Life does not give you all the answers ahead of time. Life does not fill in all the blanks for you. Neither does God.

Sometimes, you have to begin not exactly knowing how it is all going to work out. Life has a degree of uncertainty that is always present. To progress, you must become comfortable with uncertainty, and you must instill that in the people you lead.

Consider the example of Abram in Genesis 12:1-4. Abram obeyed when God told him to leave his country, family, and father's house to go to a land that God would show him. There is no record that Abram asked God for any details before departing. He simply trusted God enough to begin, and God blessed him, helping him in his journey to the Land of Promise. The journey to the unknown land was—in reality—the journey of faith.

Many of us want to have everything mapped out. We want God to show us the entire plan. We say, "God, just give me a little snapshot of how this is all going to work out, and I will follow you." But, as you may well know, God does not work like that. God always leaves a few blanks in the sentence to stretch our faith. If He gave us all the details, I doubt that we would move at all—especially when we see the challenges we might have to endure along the way!

It is like a little kid going into a dark room. I have a son. When he was younger, and my wife or I would tell him to go upstairs and get his pajamas on, he would sometimes be a little hesitant. So, we would say to him that we would walk him to the top of the stairs and wait for him to go into his room, turn on the lights and prepare to get into bed. I would watch him after I walked him to the top of the steps. He would turn the corner, looking around with his eyes all big, taking one baby step after another. He would then look back at me, take another step, look back again, then peer into his room and try to find his light switch—one foot in the room and one foot out of the room.

That is how I see some people approach an opportunity—like a little kid walking into a dark room.

Their eyes are big, they are taking baby steps, and they have one foot in and one foot out. They want to do something, but they do not know how it will work out, so they leave one foot on the

outside so they can run—in case a monster comes out to get them! They are afraid of the unknown.

People like that seldom accomplish anything because they are scared to go after something wholeheartedly. They are afraid to do anything they have never done before. They are scared to go where they have never been before. They are afraid to have what they have never had before. Some of us have become so accustomed to our way of living, so used to our world, that when God presents an opportunity to experience something we have never experienced before, we get fearful and back up. Yet, we expect to have what we have never had before, forgetting that to have what we have never had, we have to do what we have never done! Remember, the "same old, same old" habits and strategies will produce "same old, same old" results.

Where there is fear of the unknown, there is no faith to push forward. This is why many of us—and those we lead—get stuck in our comfort zones and in unproductive cycles and predictable ways of doing things. We are afraid to have what we have never had before. Life has conditioned some of us to accept dysfunction or abuse as normal, so we lack the courage to reach for something new. We are uncertain when we mentor someone that the something new he or she experiences will not just be another setback or failure! That fear of the unknown keeps us from apprehending the breakthrough that God has for them or us. It keeps everyone

from having what they have never had and being what they have never been before.

For some of us, the fear is so great that it paralyzes us, and we lose the faith to break through. So, we stay outside the promise and never see the season of birthing new things manifest. In the end, that word, that promise, that dream we have been carrying never becomes a reality—all because of the fear of the unknown.

Some people are afraid to do what they have never done before—they do not know if they want to take the risk or put themselves in what they feel is a vulnerable position. Other people are afraid to go places they have never gone before. They are used to certain surroundings or a particular group of friends. They are used to a certain environment and doing something new requires them to go where they have never gone before. Some people are afraid to have what they have never had before. Because of their low self-esteem or self-worth, they think they are only supposed to live at a certain level. They believe they are disqualified from having anything better.

Thoughts like, *I am not worthy of this, so I am not going to pursue it,* or *I do not think I am supposed to have that, so I am afraid to accept anything beyond my current reality—afraid to be what I have never been before,* pervade their reality. You should not disqualify yourself nor allow others to disqualify themselves from better things. You must be careful how you think about yourself,

"For as [a man] thinketh in his heart, so [is] he" (Proverbs 23:7 KJV), and model proper thinking for those who look to you for guidance. Life has a way of conditioning people to survive and not thrive. After becoming conditioned, we become comfortable and complacent. At that point, many settle for being lonely, addicted, broken, dysfunctional, abused, and so on. Friend, as you are reading this book, I want to tell you loud and clear: It's time for you to break the fear of being what you have never been before. Let go of what you are accustomed to. Reject the fear of being blessed, being happy, and being free.

For too long, you have lived being someone whom God never intended for you to be. You think it is easier or less painful to remain who you have been. But each day that you continue in that existence, you lose a day experiencing a future filled with promise and possibility. You are who God says you are, and He sent Jesus so that you and those who look to you can have life and live it more abundantly (see John 10:10).

Your journey may have been difficult. You may not believe you can have a business because that would require certain qualities you do not think you possess. Maybe you are afraid to be happy in life because you have only experienced sadness. Or, perhaps you are afraid to have a healthy relationship because you have only been in dysfunctional ones. You are afraid to be free because you have only experienced bondage or captivity. You are afraid to have or to be because you have never had or been either before. If

this doesn't apply to you specifically, it may apply to those under your leadership.

All these fears of the unknown abound, but if you are going to break through, you have to say to yourself, "You know what? Even though I have never experienced it, even though I have never tasted it, even though I have never lived it, I am not afraid to go there—I am not afraid of the unknown because Christ, my 'older brother' Zerah, has already gone before me. And, since Christ is my savior and friend, and His hand has already been to my unknown, my unknown is not a bottomless pit that is going to swallow me up."

This we know because Jeremiah 29:11 (NKJV) further states, "For I know the thoughts that I think toward you, says the LORD, thoughts of peace, and not of evil, to give you an expected end." I do not know about you, but when I think of "an expected end," I think of good, rather than bad, outcomes. Do you know of any parents who wish that their child fails in life? No. The vast majority of parents expect good things for their children. If so, why should you expect bad things for yourself or those who you lead if you both step out in faith? Why do you expect that what is around the corner is bad? Why not good? More importantly, if God thinks good thoughts toward you, you should not let the enemy convince you that your unknown outcome is terrible.

It is true: Life is not a bed of roses. But, it is also true that most of our fears never even materialize. So, step forward in faith since we serve a good God who desires good outcomes for our lives for His name's sake and glory. This is why He has "thoughts of peace, and not of evil" for those who follow Him. Like Perez, you may have to break through into the unknown world outside the womb, screaming and kicking as you go, only to find an outside world that is full of unlimited potential! Then, you will wonder why you waited so long to break through!

> *You gain strength, courage, and confidence by every experience in which you really stop to look fear in the face. You must do the thing you think you cannot do.*
> —Eleanor Roosevelt[8]

It is dangerous to become comfortable with your current condition or position because there is much more available! If you believe that your current condition is normal, you will lack the tenacity, courage, fortitude, and boldness to change it. If you are convinced that where you are in life is the best that it will ever be, you will settle for that. Your followers will do the same. If you begin to think that it is just your lot in life, and you are supposed just to accept it, or that you are never going to see a brighter day or experience more than you have right now, then guess what? Your low expectations will come to pass. You will continue to experience

---

8 "Eleanor Roosevelt," FDR Presidential Library & Museum, accessed December 21, 2010, https://www.fdrlibrary.org/eleanor-roosevelt.

only what you are experiencing now! Get ready to continue living your life under those same low ceilings.

This is the reason so many people are frustrated and dissatisfied with life. They feel trapped by their own existence. They have become imprisoned by the limitations of their thinking and imaginations. There ought to be something in you that is always reaching, always stretching, striving for something more. People will see your courage and emulate it in *their own* lives.

Now, do not get me wrong. I am not talking about being ungrateful or discontented. I believe you should be thankful, happy, and content— but you should be determined that you will not stay where you are forever—especially when Zerah (Christ) has gone before you and made a way for you! Remember that Christ is the *Alpha* (beginning) and the *Omega* (end) of your life (see Revelation 1:8). There are no unknowns with God (see 1 John 3:20 and John 16:30). So, step out in faith, knowing that you'll never outrun Him. Just like Zerah, His hand is always ahead of you. The unknown calamity that keeps you from stepping out in faith will have to deal with Him first before it reaches you. Comforting, isn't it? Can you hear Him telling you, like he told the Israelites in Isaiah 54:5 (NIV), "Fear not?" I hope so. And share that gentle instruction with those you lead.

PRACTICAL POINTS: BREAKING THE FEAR OF THE UNKNOWNS

To overcome the fear of the unknown, breakthrough people take several action steps:

FIRST, THEY IDENTIFY WHERE THIS FEAR EXISTS IN THEIR LIVES.

They are aware of where it shows up and how it hinders their progress. Breakthrough people are brave enough to admit and face the fear. Only after people locate the fear are they able to eradicate the fear. All too often, we make excuses and rationalize our way out of confronting the unknown. We convince ourselves that it is easier and less painful to deny or just avoid it. Recognize how this fear manifests in your life? Where does it hinder progress in your life? What opportunities have you missed out on as a result of not confronting this fear?

SECOND, THEY REFLECT ON WHAT MAKES THEM UNCOMFORTABLE ABOUT FACING THE FEAR.

For example, some people stay in a dysfunctional relationship that negatively impacts them because they believe that this is better than not having a relationship. In this scenario, the real fear is being alone. Friend, if you find yourself in such a relationship and have chosen just to accept it, there is a possibility that the thought of being by yourself terrifies you. The unknown of being alone

has trapped you in a bad situation. Get to the root of what makes you afraid and deal with the real issue.

THIRD, BREAKTHROUGH PEOPLE LOOK AT THE UNKNOWN OBJECTIVELY.

If you look at the unknown subjectively, you will see it only through your insecurities and limitations and end up creating negative outcomes in your mind. Instead, learn to look at the unknown objectively. Look at others who have faced the same unknown and have achieved triumphant outcomes.

Others have often faced the same uncertainties and even greater, yet they stepped out with boldness into the unknown and made remarkable accomplishments. If you have not summoned the courage yet, look for examples from others who have faced the fear of the unknown and overcome. Let their stories and victories inspire you. If Neil Armstrong could walk on the moon, there must be a star up there waiting on you!

FINALLY, BREAKTHROUGH PEOPLE DECIDE TO TAKE ACTION.

Determine what you can do, and do it. You cannot allow the fear of the unknown to master you. You must master it. The first step to taking action is developing a plan. List each step that you need to take to move forward.

Do not be overwhelmed by the size of the matter at hand. Take it one step at a time. As the African proverb says, "The way that you eat an elephant is by taking one bite at a time!" Choose to walk out of the limitations of your mind, doing what you have never done before, going where you have never gone before, having what you have never had before, and being what you have never been before. It doesn't happen overnight, but it does begin for each of us with a step.

QUESTIONS FOR REFLECTION

**ASK YOURSELF OR THOSE YOU LEAD,
MENTOR, OR COUNSEL:**

- What about the unknown is terrifying? How has it hindered your life and your ability to take action?

- Make a list of specific instances when the "fear of the unknown" caused you to draw back, only to realize later that you should have moved forward.

- Make a list of specific instances when the "fear of the unknown" caused you to draw back, only to realize later that you were right to stay put.

- Which of the above lists is longer? My guess is that the first list is longer.

- Of the things that you should have acted on, which ones are still doable?

- What do you plan to do about the things that are still doable?

- In the instances that you drew back, what was the root of the fear?

- What do you need to do to face the causes of those fears head-on?

- In what activities can you purposefully engage to push yourself outside of your comfort zone and on to greater achievements in life?

CHAPTER 3

THE FEAR OF FAILURE

Success is not final, and failure never
fatal. It's courage that counts.
—George F. Tilton [9]

For though the righteous fall seven times, they rise again.
— Proverbs 24:16 (NIV)

The late Steve Jobs possessed perhaps one of this generation's most brilliant and innovative minds. Along with his business partner Steve Wozniak, he is credited by many to have revolutionized the computer industry. Together they produced a series of user-friendly personal computers that were initially marketed at $666.66 each. Their first model, the Apple I, earned $774,000. Three years later, after the release of the Apple II, sales increased 700 percent to $139 million. In 1980, on its first day of being a publicly-traded company, Apple Computer's market value

9   Forbes. *Forbes Magazine*. Accessed April 15, 2021. https://www.forbes.com/quotes/3475/.

was $1.2 billion. Over the next several years, one innovative idea after another was conceived. One revolutionary product after another was rolled out. The MacBook Air, iPod, iPhone, iPad, and iTunes radically changed the world of technology. In 2010, Apple's market value was over $200 billion. However, this incredible story of growth and business success did not start in grand fashion.

Steve Jobs was born in 1955 to two University of Wisconsin graduate students who gave him up for adoption.[10] He was adopted as an infant.[11] Growing up, Jobs worked with his father on electronics in the family garage. Constantly frustrated by formal education, he went to Reed College after high school, though he dropped out after six months. Later, Jobs began designing video games for Atari. In 1976, at the age of 21, he and Wozniak started Apple Computer in the Jobs' family garage.[12] They financed this business endeavor after Jobs sold his Volkswagen bus and Wozniak sold his treasured scientific calculator. Their initial product was the Apple I. Jobs was still working for Atari and Wozniak for Hewlett Packard. They both tried to sell their design of this kit computer to their respective employers. Both of them were refused and failed in their first attempt to sell their first idea.

10 "Steve Jobs." Biography.com. A&E Networks Television, February 4, 2021. https://www.biography.com/business-figure/steve-jobs.

11 "Steve Jobs and Steve Wozniak." Lemelson. Accessed November 13, 2011. https://lemelson.mit.edu/resources/steve-jobs-and-steve-wozniak.

12 "Short Bio: All about Steve Jobs.com," Short Bio | all about Steve Jobs.com, accessed March 28, 2012, http://allaboutstevejobs.com/bio/longbio_01.php.

This is not the beginning one would expect for a company that has had such remarkable impact on our generation and has accumulated more cash reserves than the US government. Some would look at this story and see failure written all over it. However, this story epitomizes the concept that failure is no indication of future defeat or success. The outcome—regardless of a person's position—all depends on what he or she does with the failure. Jobs could have quit after finding out he was adopted. He could have quit after having been frustrated in high school. He could have walked away after he dropped out of college. He could have given up on his dream after both Atari and Hewlett Packard told him and his business partner, "No, we are not interested." Instead of quitting, he allowed these "failures" to fuel him forward to breakthrough.

Society has put such a stigma on failure. Somehow, if you fail, you are disqualified. If you fail, you are no good. Failure is an indictment against you. There must be something wrong with you; otherwise, you never would have failed. Especially as leaders, because of this stigma—as if failure were the end-all, the nail in the coffin—we develop a fear of it. But, when we look at life and observe history, we see that individuals who have done remarkable things failed many times. Just like Steve Jobs and many others. How many times did Edison fail before he got the light bulb right? How many times did Ford fail before he finally got his car company to succeed? How many times did Roger Bannister try to run a four-minute mile before he actually did it?

We cannot allow society's stigma of failure to build in us a fear of failure. If we as leaders allow this to happen, what hope do those who look to us have? Many of those who stigmatize failure have never done anything, which disqualifies them from criticizing those who are trying.

I have found that most people who have tried to do something tend to be encouraging to those who are also trying because they know the effort it takes to succeed. On the other hand, the under-achievers in life criticize the achievers in life out of jealousy. So, the next time someone criticizes your failures, check them out first to see if they are qualified to criticize you. If not, do not pay undue attention to them.

As Thomas Edison once said, "Many of life's failures are men who did not realize how close they were to success when they gave up."[13] They were right there at the threshold before they gave up—right there before the doorway of success. They were right there on the edge of seeing all of their work, toil, labor, sweat, and effort pay off—and then they gave up! They quit just before they saw the payoff. They threw in the towel just before they got the victory. They walked away from it just at the time they were getting ready to step over into the very thing that they had been dreaming of. What a tragedy! To quote Edison again, "Nearly every man who develops an idea works it up to the point where it looks impossible, and then he gets discouraged." That is not the

---

place to become discouraged because "perseverance is a great element of success. If you only knock long enough and loud enough at the gate, you are sure to wake up somebody."[14]

There will be times, seasons, and moments when we feel like quitting, when we feel like giving up, when we feel like we cannot go another step. We cannot take it another day; we are riddled with doubt in our minds, we have too many worries and concerns, we do not think it is worth it, we do not think it is ever going to pan out, and we are ready to just quit. When you feel that way, or your heart aches for a mentoree, remember Edison's quote: "Failure is only final if you quit." You have to have—and instill in others—such tenacity on the inside that you vow to never, ever give up on your dream—in spite of the resistance or opposition. In spite of the struggle or challenge—never give up on your dream. The next phone call or the next event could be the very opportunity that turns it all around for you or allows you to turn it around for someone else.

Failure is only final if one quits. If you say you are going to get back up, even if you took one on the chin, got egg on your face, or slipped up, if you refuse to let failure be final for you, that incident becomes a stepping-stone for you; not a tombstone, a stepping-stone.

---

14 "Henry Wadsworth Longfellow Quotes." BrainyQuote. Xplore. Accessed April 15, 2021. https://www.brainyquote.com/quotes/henry_wadsworth_longfello_124652.

The Bible says that a righteous man, though he falls seven times, will get back up (see Proverbs 24:16). I've often wondered why this man is considered righteous if he keeps falling. If you keep messing up and making mistakes, how can you be considered righteous? I think the key is that he keeps getting back up. He yet believes that even though he falls more than once or twice or even many times, he can still get back up. He keeps getting up because he knows who has gone before him and secured the victory for him. Since God is on his side, he can stand up every time he's knocked down because he knows that failure does not mean that God has abandoned him. It may very well be the evidence that God is with him. Being knocked down simply means he is in a battle. Refusing to stay down is actually an expression of faith in the ability of God to restore and strengthen us. Let us not think any differently toward those who follow us!

Conversely, staying down is an expression of doubt in God's ability to bring us through difficult situations, and the consequences of this can be dire. As the Bible teaches (see Hebrews 10:39), those that shrink back from the fight get destroyed, while those that keep the faith and keep rising despite the blows get saved. We sometimes think that staying down and making peace with failure will preserve our lives when, in fact, doing so is tantamount to signing a contract with failure—or worse. Though you may feel like you cannot keep on and are about to quit, remember that failure is only final if you quit. As Vince Lombardi once said,

"Winners never quit, and quitters never win."[15] When it comes time to get back up from failure, we must change the way we view it. We must encourage those we mentor and coach to view it differently. A major difference between those who are achievers and those who are average is how they perceive and respond to failure. Success has many teachers. Failure just happens to be one of them. If failure is not going to be final in life, we must allow it to become a teacher. Most people hate failure because they see it as an indictment or verdict against them. They assume that failure only takes them backward. I want to suggest that if people will allow failure to teach them, it will propel them forward and not backward.

BREAKING THE FEAR OF FAILURE

Here are five things you can do to make failure work for you and not against you. Model these attitudes and watch those around you make failure work for them too.

OWN IT.

Accept your part of the failure. Take responsibility. This is powerful because in doing so, you move from being a victim to being empowered to do better next time. Fight the temptation to point the finger at others. This only robs you of the opportunity to learn from your mistakes, and it alienates you from others which is the

---

15 "A Quote by Vince Lombardi Jr." Goodreads. Goodreads. Accessed April 15, 2021. https://www.goodreads.com/quotes/458325-winners-never-quit-and-quitters-never-win.

last thing we want to do as leaders, mentors, or coaches. Nobody wants to be around someone who always blames others for his or her failures.

HIT THE DELETE BUTTON.

After learning the lessons, move on. Understand that failure is temporary. It does not have to be a permanent pit that you sit in for the rest of your life. Stop rehearsing, replaying, and reliving the failure. Instead, glean what you can from the experience and then delete from your mind and conversation all the negative emotions connected to the experience. Changing what you say is extremely important because the words you speak either give life or death to those negative emotions. People hear what we say. They say the same things to themselves. Do not continue to talk about the loss, embarrassment, or pain. When you stop speaking about it you disconnect from it. You become free to move forward from failure into a future of success, and those who hear you do too.

REJECT REJECTION.

Breakthrough people see failure as a teacher and not as a judge. They allow failure to teach them lessons but not to define their identity. Breakthrough people do not base their self-worth on their successes or failures. They live from the inside out. They do not allow their mistakes to determine who they are. They know that their worth is determined by who God has created them to be, not

by what they do. Who they are defines what they do, and not the other way around. Reject the temptation to receive rejection and negative labels from others and yourself. Protect those you lead in the same way. Failure does not define any person or indicate any person's worth. Failure should never become an identity. It is only an incident. You may have failed but you are not a failure.

WORK WHAT WORKS.

Breakthrough people learn what works and what does not work from failure. A positive result of failure is that it helps you identify what to take forward and what to leave behind. Attitudes, habits, and sometimes even people, must be identified as either vital components to your comeback or contributors to your setback. Do not waste any more time wallowing in your weakness or with those that bring you down. Highlight strengths and continue to invest in them. People have more success when they operate from their strengths instead of from their weaknesses.

RESET FOR THE REALISTIC.

A familiar song says that you have to pick yourself up, brush yourself off, and start all over again.[16] After failure, breakthrough people understand that they cannot change yesterday, but they can reset for tomorrow. Take the lessons you have learned and apply them to your new goal. But, take time to reassess your goal

16 "Jerome Ken—Pick Yourself Up." Genius. Accessed April 15, 2021. https://genius.com/Jerome-kern-pick-yourself-up-lyrics.

to make sure you are being realistic. Being unrealistic sets you up for disappointment. Once you have reset your goal, go after it with everything you have.

QUESTIONS FOR REFLECTION

**ASK YOURSELF OR THOSE YOU LEAD,
MENTOR OR COUNSEL:**

- Make a list of specific instances when the "fear of failure" prevented you from doing something that you later realized you should have done.

- For many people, the "fear of failure" is often a cover-up for specific inadequacies that they feel. What do you consider to be your greatest inadequacies?

- Some of our inadequacies relate to natural things, like not having as much education as we would like. For the inadequacies listed above, make a list of natural remedies or steps that you can take to address them. Which of these are you willing to implement?

- Some of the things we have failed in can be salvaged. Make a list of things in your life that are salvageable. What do you plan to do about those things?

- What actions from past mistakes do you need to own so that you will not repeat them?

- What new realistic expectations do you need to set to go forward?

- If, in a worst-case scenario, you chase your dreams and fall flat on your face, how long would it take to recover? (The answer is probably less than you expect.)

CHAPTER 4

THE FEAR OF GOING FIRST

If you don't risk anything, you risk even more.
—Erica Jong[17]

*". . . Then you will know which way to go, since
you have never been this way before. . . ."*
—Joshua 3:4 (NIV)

In 1961, segregation was a normal occurrence across America. For generations, the practice of denying individuals their human rights had been permitted. For centuries, access to various institutions and privileges was denied to people based on the color of their skin. No consideration was given to character, achievement, or merit. Simply based on ethnicity, people were discriminated against systematically and openly. Throughout the country, displays of segregation were perpetuated regularly.

---

17 "If You Don't Risk Anything, You Risk Even More. by Erica Jong," If you don't risk anything, you risk even more. by Erica Jong, accessed December 21, 2010, https://www. quotedb.com/quotes/1848.

This was especially true in Oxford, Mississippi, at the University of Mississippi.

On May 31, 1961, the NAACP Legal Defense and Educational Fund filed a lawsuit in the US District Court claiming that the university had denied James Meredith admittance solely because he was African American, even though his academic record had been exemplary.[18]

Meredith was a bright and intelligent student. He had attended Jackson State University for two years. Later he would study political science at the University of Ibadan in Nigeria, Africa. Through a scholarship, he would attend law school at Columbia University and earn a law degree. He was not only smart; he was an activist who had the courage and fortitude to fight for people's rights. He organized and led a civil rights march, the "March Against Fear" from Memphis, Tennessee, to Jackson, Mississippi, in June 1966. It was a public demonstration to rally blacks to register and vote after the Voting Rights Act of 1965 had passed. The Voting Rights Act was to guarantee federal enforcement of those rights. He wanted to encourage blacks to overcome fear of violence at the polls. It was during this event that he was shot. However, he recovered from his wounds and rejoined the march before it reached Jackson. This event resulted in 4,000 black Mississippi residents registering to vote.

---

18 Meredith, James. *Three Years in Mississippi*. Bloomington, IN: Indiana University Press, 1966.

Inspired by President Kennedy's inaugural address, Meredith decided to exercise his constitutional rights and apply to the University of Mississippi. His objective was to force the President to enforce civil rights for African Americans. The US Supreme Court had ruled in the *Brown v. Board of Education (1955)* decision that publicly supported schools had to be desegregated. Though the University of Mississippi, under the state's legally imposed racial segregation, had traditionally accepted only white students, he was determined to be the first African American to attend the university. Meredith said, "Nobody handpicked me. I believe, and believe now, that I have a Divine Responsibility. . . . I am familiar with probable difficulties involved in such a move as I am undertaking and I am fully prepared to pursue it all the way to a degree from the University of Mississippi."[19] Twice he was denied.

The case filed by the NAACP Legal Defense and Educational Fund in the US District Court on May 31, 1961, went all the way to the US Supreme Court. It ruled that Meredith had the right to be admitted to the school. Despite being legally entitled to register, the Governor of Mississippi, Ross Barnett, tried to block him by having the legislature pass a law that "prohibited any person who was convicted of a state crime from admission to a state school." The law was directed at Meredith, who had been convicted of "false voter registrations." In response to this action, US Attorney General Robert F. Kennedy consulted with Governor Barnett, who

---

19 Meredith, James. *Three Years in Mississippi*. Bloomington, IN: Indiana University Press, 1966.

later agreed to have Meredith enroll in the university.[20] White students and anti-desegregation supporters protested his enrollment by rioting on the Oxford campus, but on October 1, 1962, James Meredith became the first African American student at the University of Mississippi.[21]

If you are going to walk in that next dimension of success and fulfillment—which all leaders strive to do—you cannot be afraid of going first. Many times, breakthrough requires us to go first. Here is the deal: If you are afraid to go first, the best you can ever be is second. You will never be first, and people don't follow the person following the first person! I know it is not deep, but it is true. The reason those who *become* first *are* first is because they are not afraid of being first. The problem, however, is that when you go first, there is no role model, no blueprint, and no precedent. You are it. So, to be first requires courage, confidence, and faith to step out and do something that may not have been done before. Just like James Meredith, you may be the first: the first believer in your family, the first business owner or college graduate, or the first to live free from addiction or abuse. It takes boldness to step out where no one has stepped out before. But just because it has not been done before does not mean it cannot be done. Anything is possible if we just allow ourselves to believe and break the fear of going first.

20 Eagles, C. *The Price of Defiance: James Meredith and the Integration of Ole Miss.* Chapel Hill, NC: The University of North Carolina Press, 2009.

21 Hendrickson, Paul. *Sons of Mississippi: a Story of Race and Its Legacy.* New York, NY: Knopf, 2003.

Have you ever thought about Peter walking on water? Other than the Lord Jesus Christ, Peter was the only person to ever walk on water; there is no record of anyone even attempting to do that. Peter could not look at anybody or recall anybody ever having done that before. He was the first one. He was in the boat with the other disciples, surrounded by water, and he thought to himself: *You know what? I think I am going to walk on the water. No one has ever done this before; it is not recorded anywhere. I have not heard this; I have not seen this. It is not on YouTube; there is no "Walking on Water for Dummies" book. Yet, I believe it is possible. I can do it!* So, he ended up doing what nobody had ever done in history—he walked on water!

In your life and in the lives of those you lead, doors will open, and opportunities will present themselves. When that happens, do not be afraid to go first. Seize the opportunity and refuse to let the fear of going first keep you in the boat of limitation. Be the one people look to—the one people recall!

I have loved golf since I was a kid, and I love watching the Masters, one of the four major international golf tournaments played each year. It is beautiful to watch, and, for me, it signals the beginning of spring. The flowers are blooming; the grass is green—it is incredible!

One year, a golfer was participating who had never won a major tournament even though he had been on the PGA Tour for many

years. It came down to the end of the tournament, and he had a two-stroke lead. All he had to do was par the 17th and 18th holes, and he would win his first major tournament—he would get the green jacket, the trophy, and the big check. His name would go down in history as the winner of that year's Masters. Instead, he choked on the 17th hole and lost one stroke from his two-stroke lead. When he went to the 18th hole, he was only ahead by one. Once again, he choked and lost his one-stroke lead. This caused him to be in a tie. Now the tournament had to be decided by a playoff, which he ultimately lost. He missed his opportunity to win the Masters.

When reporters interviewed him afterward, they asked him what was going through his mind when he teed off at the 17th hole, when all he had to do to win was avoid making a mistake. His response? He started thinking about the fact that he had never done it before—he had never had the lead in a major tournament before. By all accounts, he was afraid of finishing first.

You have to understand that the people who come in first are not afraid of being first! You have to believe—without a shadow of a doubt—that you deserve to be first, that you are supposed to win, be a champion, overcome, and break through. And you must encourage others to believe it too!

When I say that we must believe that we are supposed to break through or deserve to be first, this is not based on us. It is not based on our qualifications or lack thereof. It is based on the fact that

Jesus already made a way for us to win. It is because of what He has done for us—you, me, and people who look to us—that we deserve to win. It is simply His grace paving the way.

However, if you somehow have it in your mind that you are not supposed to win, then guess what? You won't. If you somehow think that you do not deserve to be first, you will find a way to prevent yourself from becoming first. Remember, if you are afraid to go first, the best you can ever be is second. If you are afraid, first is no longer an option; first is no longer something you can strive for because, in your mind, you have already relegated yourself to losing.

The challenge of going first is that it gives you something to carve out, something to venture out into, not knowing exactly how it will happen, when it is going to happen, or how it is all going to work. Going first means you have to pave the way. Sometimes, that is where we get stuck. But, think of those individuals who have broken through. They did not have anybody to model how it was supposed to work for them, which is exactly how they became leaders. Next time, take courage and go forward because Zerah's hand, even Christ's, has already gone before you and made a way for you.

Uncertainty and mystery are energies of life.
Do not let them scare you unduly, for they keep
the boredom at bay and spark creativity.
—R. I. Fitzhenry [22]

When there is no model or precedent, people must unlock the creativity and the innovation that lives within them. To unlock it, they must first recognize that it is there. When they devalue and dismiss it, and we as leaders are not there to correct that, that resourcefulness is sentenced to die. They think it belongs only to those who are professional musicians, artists, or inventors—or professional coaches, trainers, and mentors. But, there is a creative and innovative dynamic inside of everyone.

The One who created us is the Creator—we have been made in His image and His likeness. That means a little bit of Him is in each of us. And if He can create, we can create. If He can innovate, we can innovate. Great ideas are in us, just waiting to get out. The problem is that we dismiss, devalue, or discount them because we somehow think that our ideas are not as good as somebody else's or that our abilities are not as special as somebody else's.

Comparison is the preoccupation of the fearful. Comparing yourself or tolerating it when your mentees compare themselves with others is generated by the fear that you are not capable or good

---

22 Fitzhenry: Uncertainty and mystery are energies of life. Don't let them scare you unduly, for they keep boredom at bay and spark creativity. Accessed April 15, 2021. https://www.quotes.net/quote/13013.

enough. You say to yourself, *That will never work. That is not a good idea. I do not know what I was thinking,* or *That will never happen.* And, of course, this becomes a self-fulfilling prophecy. To break through, you must believe that creativity and innovation dwell on the inside of us "for the gifts and the calling of God are irrevocable" (Romans 11:29, ESV).

Those ideas are there for a reason. Value them! Pursue them! Begin to move on them! To overcome the fear of going first, we have to believe that God has already gone before you and charted your destiny. Unlock the creativity that lives inside you and the people you lead, and go after the dream and the vision that He has placed in your heart. Remember this: Not only has He gone before and made a way for you; He is also with you as you take that journey.

PRACTICAL POINTS: BREAKING THE FEAR OF GOING FIRST

To break the fear of going first, consider these points:

DO NOT DISMISS YOUR IDEAS PREMATURELY.

Take note of your impulses and inclinations. Breakthrough people are sensitive to their internal promptings, and they encourage others to also be aware of their own. These may come in the form of ideas, desires, questions, or imaginations. Many times, they provide the spark to begin a journey of exploring new realities. The

trap we must avoid is that of dismissing ideas prematurely. Once we do this, it becomes easy to hit the delete button and discard what may have been a door opener. Instead, write down or record those internal promptings so that they can be explored further.

ASK QUESTIONS AND DO SOME RESEARCH.

I have observed that breakthrough people ask great questions of themselves and others. If you do not ask questions, you will not discover answers.

Most inventions began with a question: What would it be like if…? How can I…? Is it possible to…? Questions are solutions in seed form. It is only through wrestling with the questions of your present experience that you can tap into the possibilities of tomorrow.

What would life be like if you got your degree or started a business? How might your follower's lives be different if they changed their associations, pursued their dreams? The Bible contains many instances where God asked people questions. It is not because He does not know the answers, but because He is prompting them to find the answers He has already provided for them.

Uncertainty can increase anxiety. When people have incomplete information, potential outcomes are unclear. This lack of clarity causes worry. Worry disempowers. Knowledge is power. Asking

the right questions enhances your research and leads you down the path of making sound decisions and helping others do the same. Reduce the anxiety by increasing your knowledge about the situation. Research all the potential outcomes, both good and bad, so everyone really understands the risks and rewards.

DREAM ABOUT THE FUTURE AND BE OPEN TO CHANGE.

A dream is powerful. It is the vehicle that breakthrough people use to travel beyond their present circumstances, limitations and barriers.

It can transport you to places beyond your current existence. First, begin to dream and use your imagination to create a mental picture of a better tomorrow. Second, determine your ideal setting for making that dream a reality. Third, define your goals and formulate your plan of action. Teach your people that success comes by following this order. Frustration comes when people get these steps out of order. Formulating action plans *before* people know where they want to go just sets them up for frustration. They then get stuck and start "spinning their wheels" in a lack of productivity.

You must open yourself up to change. It is pointless to dream of a better tomorrow if you are not willing to consider that there is a better way. Begin to see that there are options. Taking risks

requires embracing change, which opens the door to new possibilities. As long as you refuse to change, you close the door to experiencing outcomes beyond your current existence.

DISMISS FAULTY ASSUMPTIONS AND BREAK FREE FROM THE APPROVAL OF OTHERS.

One of the most significant roadblocks to one's ability to dream and envision a better future is relying on faulty assumptions. They cause us to be swayed by unsubstantiated fears and scenarios. Such assumptions cause us to become barrier-conscious and to be preoccupied with limitations. Breakthrough people do not rely on faulty assumptions that hinder their ability to think outside the box. For us to break through, we must begin to challenge faulty assumptions and dismiss them.

Remember: Those who are going to be first cannot wait until everyone approves of their decisions. Most people are comfortable with where you are currently, but they begin to get uncomfortable when you start pursuing your dreams. Do not let the opinion of others paralyze your progress.

CONSIDER THE COST OF MISSED OPPORTUNITIES.

Opportunities are often preceded by risks and obstacles. Thus, if you and the people who follow you do not take risks, you cannot apprehend the hidden opportunities. There is a risk in not taking

a risk! In failing to take a risk, you risk losing future success, achievement, and fulfillment. You forfeit your chance to make a difference and live out your purpose in your own life and in the lives of others. By counting the cost of missed opportunities, you will realize that you and yours stand to gain so much more by taking the risk.

QUESTIONS FOR REFLECTION

ASK YOURSELF OR THOSE YOU LEAD, MENTOR OR COUNSEL:

- How does the fear of going first manifest in your life?

- Write down a list of your dreams.

- Write down specific times when doors opened in your life, and you drew back because you were afraid of going first.

- What did your drawing back cost you?

- Since God is a God of second chances, ask Him for the courage to move forward next time He opens a door for you. Write down your action plan for moving forward the next time you see an open door.

- List the talents and abilities that you possess. How can you apply and use them better? What internal promptings do you need to act on?

- What faulty assumptions are possibly holding you back? How will you begin to challenge them?

CHAPTER 5

THE FEAR OF INVESTMENT

*Opportunity is missed by most people
because it comes dressed in overalls and looks like work.*
—Thomas Edison [23]

Whoever does not want to work should not be allowed to eat.
—2 Thessalonians 3:10 (GW)

At the age of eighteen, a young girl named Agnes left home. She would never see her mother or sister again.[24] During the years prior, this girl had been intrigued by stories of missionaries and their service in Bengal. By the age of twelve, she was convinced that she should devote herself to religious life. She took her first religious vows on May 24, 1931. At that time, she chose to be named after Theresa de Lisieux, the patron saint of missionaries.

---

23 "Thomas A. Edison Quotes." BrainyQuote. Xplore. Accessed April 15, 2021. https://www.brainyquote.com/quotes/thomas_a_edison_104931.

24 Sebba, Anne. *Mother Teresa: Beyond the Image.* New York, NY: Doubleday Religion, 1997.

Another nun, however, had already chosen that name, so Agnes selected the Spanish spelling of Teresa.

After taking her solemn vows in 1937, Teresa served twelve years as a teacher in a school in eastern Calcutta. The Bengal Famine of 1943 brought great misery and despair to the city of Calcutta and surrounding areas. This event, along with the Hindu/Muslim violence in 1946, brought pronounced devastation and poverty. These desperate conditions would change the course of Teresa's life. In 1940, Teresa experienced what she later described as "the call within the call" while traveling by train to her annual retreat.[25] "I was to leave the convent and help the poor while living among them. It was an order. To fail would have been to break the faith."

While on that train ride, viewing the poverty and suffering left such a deep impression that she asked for permission from her superiors to leave the convent school and follow the call to work among the poor. She invested her life in working and serving the poorest of the poor in the slums of Calcutta. Although she had no financial support, she depended on Divine Providence and started an open-air school for the slum children. At the beginning of 1949, she was joined in her effort by a group of young women and laid the foundation of a new religious community to help the outcast.

Teresa wrote in her diary that her first year was fraught with difficulties. She had no income and had to resort to begging for food

25 Spink, K. *Mother Teresa: A Complete Authorized Biography.* New York, NY: HarperCollins, 1997.

supplies. Teresa experienced doubt, loneliness, and the temptation to return to the comfort of convent life during the early months.

In 1950, the Vatican gave Teresa permission to start the order that would later be called the Missionaries of Charity. It began with thirteen members. According to Teresa, its mission was to care for "the hungry, the naked, the homeless, the crippled, the blind, the lepers and those people who feel unwanted, unloved, uncared for throughout society—the people that have become a burden to the society and are shunned by everyone."

For forty-five years, Teresa worked and invested herself in this mission. This once small order of a few women continued to grow and have a tremendous impact all over the world. Teresa later became known as Mother Teresa. In 1979, she won the Nobel Peace Prize.[26] At the time of her death, the Missionaries of Charity had 610 missions in 123 countries, including hospices and homes for people with HIV/AIDS, leprosy, and tuberculosis, soup kitchens, children and family counseling programs, orphanages, and schools.

Mother Teresa was motivated by a heart of compassion to work in areas no one else worked in—for people who had been forgotten about by most of society. She understood that if she were going to make a difference, she had to be willing to invest all that she had—even when it looked like it was not worth it. Because she

26 Graff Clucas, J. *Mother Teresa (World Leaders Past and Present)*. New York, NY: Chelsea House Publishing, 1998.

overcame the fear to invest, she broke through and became a heroine to many all over the world.

If you are going to stay where you are, if you are content, and if you just want to camp out in your current set of circumstances, do not worry about work. However, if you want to move to the next dimension, if you want to see another level of fulfillment, and if you want to lead others who will grow to lead others, you cannot be afraid of investing yourself through work. The blessing and favor of God do not always mean that things are going to happen automatically for you. Just because you have a promise does not mean that promise is just going to waltz into your life. The opportunities for success are available, but success is not automatic. Mother Teresa had an opportunity to make a difference, but it required a significant investment of sacrifice. If you are going to make the most of the opportunities that lie ahead, you must invest yourself in your future and the futures of others by being willing to work.

I could go to the best gymnasium or workout facility, one that has weights, treadmills, ellipticals, saunas, and so on. I could have access to all this equipment and have a personal trainer, too. I could come back and tell you how I signed up and give you all the details about how exciting and elaborate this gym is. But, five months later, the real question would be, "How many times did you go to the gym and use the equipment?" That is all that matters.

So, even when I have access to the opportunity, I still have to put in the work to get the results I need. Success is available, but not automatic. As Proverbs 20:4 (NLT) says, "Those too lazy to plow in the right season will have no food at the harvest." And, it's very possible—if these people were given food—that a few chapters later, Proverbs 26:15 (NLT) would describe them again: "Lazy people take food in their hand but do not even lift it to their mouth." Work causes us to hold onto the promises of God to a much greater extent than if everything were just handed to us. Easy come, easy go. As leaders, you know that when you put some sweat and tears into something, you will value it more than if it were free for the taking. So many times when opposition comes, people are tempted to pull back instead of getting in there and putting a shoulder to the plow and working until they see the manifestation of what God has promised in their lives. Especially as a leader, you have to work with what God has given you. Work your faith. Work your knowledge. Work your talents. Get in there and make it happen! Invest in your future. You cannot be afraid to fight for what God has promised you because you are fighting for His promises to others also. Work is a prophetic act. When you invest your time and talent into your dream, it demonstrates your belief that it will become a reality.

Think about David. At a very early age, he was anointed to be king over Israel—it was his destiny. But just after he was anointed by Samuel, he went right back to work caring for the sheep in the field. The kingship did not happen overnight, with

the twinkle of an eye, nor at the snap of his fingers. It took a little time. It involved a process, and during that process, David was out there working. He tended the sheep, and fought both a lion and a bear, which prepared him for the well-known battle during which he killed a giant named Goliath. In order for David to walk in the fulfillment of the promise, he had to be willing to fight for his promise.

Along the journey, he had to fight against those distractions and powers that tried to steal, kill, and destroy what belonged to him. Our journey is the same. We, too, will have to fight against those things that will try to steal, kill, and destroy our confidence, talent, promise, and desire. The life of Mother Teresa demonstrates this. Every struggle and hardship prepared her to have even greater impact. With each battle that we win, those in our spheres of influence will also win, as we gain the strength and experience needed to equip us for the next step in the process.

Our perspective concerning the process, then, must be altered. The process is not something to just endure; it is something to value. It is an investment. It is through process that the essentials of our success are developed—intangibles such as character, integrity, guts, tenacity, and so on. Some things in life we cannot get by reading a book or listening to a podcast. You have to go through something. You have to walk it out and work it out. Not only does the process develop positive traits in us, it also removes negative characteristics from us: pride, inconsistency, laziness, and much

more. Too many times, we are so consumed with getting to the promise that we pout about the process. Learn to appreciate the process. Communicate that it is preparing you not only to arrive at the promise but also to possess it.

There are promises in my life that I have been in pursuit of for years, but they have not materialized yet, and I am sure you could say the same thing. The temptation is to quit believing and stop pushing forward, but I have learned that with each step, I am getting stronger, I am getting bigger, and I am getting better. I am being prepared to not simply arrive but to occupy the place that God has destined for me. We must understand that many times, work is the process that God uses to prepare us for the break-through. God wants us to succeed, but He is even more interested in conforming us to the image of Christ.

One of the reasons many have a fear of work is because it requires investment. It involves a cost. A price has to be paid for every accomplishment. Success is not cheap—it demands sacrifice. The principle is that you cannot expect a harvest where you have not first sown. Frustration and disappointment are the results of not remembering this principle. We all know people who attempt to reap where they have not sown. If you want to see change or fruit-fulness in any area of your life, whether it be relational, physical, financial, or spiritual, you will have to sow into that area. It is just like the bank account that requires deposits before withdrawals can be made. Many of us are trying to make withdrawals from

areas of our lives where we have not invested. So we keep getting a big NSF—Non-Sufficient Funds—all because we did not invest and sow.

This reluctance to sow may stem from the pain of former failures and past disappointments. Shame, guilt, loss, or embarrassment over yesterday may make us question whether or not making an investment today will be worth it. We may find ourselves or hear others saying, "The last time I did this, it did not work," or "The last time I did this, I looked like a fool," or "The last time I did this, I fell on my face," or "The last time I said this was going to happen, it did not happen." These feelings make people reluctant to consistently invest their time, talent, and resources. So, when another opportunity comes along, they miss it.

For any opportunity to benefit us, we must completely and totally invest ourselves in it; otherwise, we will not see the results we desire. Even when we are disappointed, we must learn from the experience, determine to get better, and move on.

For some of you, the reason you have not totally invested, the reason you are out on the fringes, or the reason you are half-in and half-out in your commitment is because of the pain of your past defeats. You are a human investing in other humans. Setbacks are inevitable. However, for you to succeed, you must learn to look forward and not backward. You have to work what you have! Some have great communication skills, administrative skills,

organizational skills, or sales abilities. Whatever it is, you have to work it! Never underestimate the value of what you have—it may be the key to your breakthrough. Remember that every time you use what you've been given, it gets stronger and propels you toward success.

Leaders cannot just have an aptitude and not use it. If you do not use it, you will lose it. Recall that I could have that gym membership, but it does me no good unless I get in there and do something with it. The talents, the abilities, and the gifts that you have are useless if they are not utilized to benefit yourself and others. At the end of the day, you may have great intentions, but you still have to take the opportunity you are given and invest in it. You can have abundant information, resources, and opportunities, but if you do not take all of them and begin to work each of them, they will not amount to much for anyone.

Instead of reveling in potential, we must learn to celebrate results and the achievements and those of others. Most people celebrate potential, the possibility that something can happen. But, potential is just that—it is made up of possibilities and opportunities. Leaders seize these moments and maximize these opportunities to achieve results. They take advantage of their situations and leave nothing to chance. Do not get caught up in celebrating potential—it is great, but it has to be transferred, translated, and turned into results. This is what you must celebrate.

You cannot move from potential to triumph if you do not believe that you can achieve! Do not celebrate just having an idea or a dream—that is where you are supposed to start, but that is not where you are supposed to stay! Dreams, visions, and ideas are awesome, but they are useless if they are not pursued and implemented. At some point, leaders have to decide, "This is it! I am living my dream. I am walking in my vision. I am going to experience this thing!" The potential of having a flourishing business is great. Actually, having one is even better. The potential of having a successful marriage is great. Having one is even better. The potential of being a success is great. Being successful is even better. Do not be afraid to sow because of what happened in the past. Invest today, and your reward will be worth it tomorrow.

PRACTICAL POINTS: BREAKING THE FEAR OF INVESTMENT

Overcoming the fear of work and investment requires seeing them differently. Breakthrough leaders have a perception of work that is positive, not negative. Their approach to it is purposeful and intentional. They do not see it as something they have to do. They see it as a necessary tool for building their dreams. Consider these useful points.

HAVE AN ATTACK ATTITUDE.

The modus operandi of how breakthrough people approach work is that they attack it. They go after it with everything they have. They are fully invested and determined. When you do not approach work with this attack mentality, it is easy for procrastination to creep in, and it's not long before that is evident to everyone around you. You say, "Oh, I'll get to that tomorrow or the next time." The problem is that procrastination robs you of time and realizing your potential. When you become infected with the disease of procrastination, excuses become your best friend, and your influence wanes. Why put off until tomorrow what you can accomplish today? Stir up the courage within you to start now!

SHARPEN YOUR SKILLS.

Breakthrough people see work as an opportunity to develop themselves and their skills. As you engage in the process of work and self-investment, you may realize that there are things you do not know and skills you do not possess. Work provides the context in which you are able to gain knowledge and abilities. Through work, your talents and skills are perfected and made available to others.

Championship athletes apply this principle in their practices and workouts. As they push themselves during the time of preparation, they increase their likelihood for victory. They develop the

stuff that is necessary to compete at a higher level. They gain what is required to be a champion. The raw materials of talent and ability are refined for excellence. There is a champion in you! Sharpen those skills and acquire what is necessary for your success—through work.

BE RESULTS-ORIENTED.

While you are working and going through the process of development, enjoy it and squeeze everything you can out of the experience. However, do not get the process mixed up with the product. Keep your eye on the goal—the end result. This requires a trait that breakthrough people possess: focus. Along the way, many distractions and disappointments will present themselves. At these times, you have to become even more focused on your ultimate objective. It is only then that your potential truly becomes productive. Breakthrough people exhibit remarkable resolve. It is that tenacity of a bulldog to not let go until they accomplish what they set out to do that makes them successful. They also refuse to be denied achieving the outcomes they determined to see from the outset of their journeys. Breakthrough leaders must be relentless.

QUESTIONS FOR REFLECTION

**ASK YOURSELF OR THOSE YOU LEAD,
MENTOR OR COUNSEL:**

- What personal investment do you need to make so that your dreams become a reality?

- When has the fear of work kept you from your dream?

- What skills do you need to develop?

- Why are you afraid to invest yourself fully?

CHAPTER 6

THE FEAR OF OPPOSITION

Difficulty, my brethren, is the nurse of greatness.
A harsh nurse, who roughly rocks her foster
children into strength and athletic proportion.
—William Cullen Bryant [27]

"Greater is he that is in you, than he that is in the world."
—1 John 4:4 (KJV)

From 1948 to 1996, South Africa was a country that enforced a system of racial segregation. Introduced during colonial times, this oppressive system classified individuals into four racial groups: Native, White, Colored, and Asian. In 1970, those who were non-white had their political representation eliminated. This inhumane system known as apartheid allowed the government to segregate beaches, education, medical care, and other public services and left non-whites with inferior facilities. During the 1950s, a series of

27 William Cullen Bryant Quotes. BrainyQuote.com, BrainyMedia Inc, 2021. https://www.brainyquote.com/quotes/william_cullen_bryant_189755, accessed April 15, 2021.

popular demonstrations was met with the banning of opposition and imprisonment of anti-apartheid leaders.

One of these leaders was Nelson Mandela, born in Transkei, South Africa, on July 18, 1918. After being educated at the University College of Fort Hare[28] and the University of Witwatersrand, and qualified in law in 1942, Nelson joined the African National Congress to resist the ruling National Party's apartheid policies that opposed the freedom of all people.

Mandela's fight for freedom caused him to be imprisoned in 1962.[29] He was sentenced to five years with hard labor. While imprisoned, Nelson was accused, along with seven others, of plotting to overthrow the government by violence. As a result, all eight of these leaders were sentenced to life imprisonment.

While incarcerated, Mandela's reputation continued to grow. Many regarded him as the most significant black leader in South Africa. He was a formidable symbol of resistance to the oppressive system of apartheid. With bold tenacity, he refused to compromise his political aspiration to obtain his freedom. Through his relentless pursuit and the work of many others, they overcame the opposition, and Mandela was released from prison in February, 1990. He aggressively continued to work towards the goals that he and others had set out to accomplish almost 40 years earlier.

28 "Nelson Mandela." Biography.com. A&E Networks Television, March 2, 2021. https://www.biography.com/political-figure/nelson-mandela.

29 Sampson, A. *Mandela: The Authorized Biography*. New York, NY: Vintage, 1999.

In 1991, after being banned since 1960, the African National Congress held its first national conference and elected Mandela as its president. His work with F. W. de Klerk to bring about the peaceful end of apartheid got the attention of the entire world, and in 1993 the Norwegian Nobel Committee awarded Mandela and de Klerk the Nobel Peace Prize. Together they had paved the way for the termination of apartheid and laid the foundation for a real democracy. In 1994, the man formerly sentenced to life in prison for his fight for freedom became president of the new democratic South Africa.[30]

After years of opposition and oppression, Nelson Mandela prevailed to see liberation for all people of South Africa. He epitomizes the power of breakthrough when the fear of opposition is defeated.

More often than not, breakthrough runs directly into opposition. The reality is, when you are in pursuit of something, when you are on your journey to that next level, that next dimension, there will be opposition. But, you cannot be afraid of it. Nelson Mandela demonstrated tremendous courage in the face of what looked like insurmountable odds. So many people miss their moment of breakthrough, because when the opposition presents itself, they shrink back. Something in them gets small, and they think the opposition is greater than the promise God has given them. As a result, they retreat and give up on their breakthrough, which, in turn, costs them and those who they lead.

30 Mandela, N. *Long Walk to Freedom: The Autobiography of Nelson Mandela* [Kindle Edition]. New York, NY: Little, Brown and Company, 1994.

Opportunity can come disguised in armor, looking like opposition. Sometimes, we focus on the disguise of opposition and begin to think that maybe what we were hoping for is not ever going to happen. We see the opposition, but we do not see the opportunity—we only see resistance. Often, opposition is there because it will produce something that you need for where you are going: faith, character, patience, strength, and so on. Instead of viewing opposition as attempting to take something from you, view it as adding to you what you need to stand in your new place.

When I was growing up, I remember my dad telling me that there were no free lunches in life—anything worth having was going to require effort to attain it. Most people—even some leaders—back up when rejection or resistance appears. Here they are with a dream, a vision, a goal, or something they are going after.

As soon as someone tells them, "You cannot do that," they take a step back. As soon as someone says, "You are not smart enough to do that; you are not gifted or talented enough," they take a step back. As soon as they hear those words of rejection, "That doesn't belong to people like you who come from where you come from," they begin to step back.

If you are going to break through and lead others to breakthrough, you have to know how to refuse to allow the voices of rejection and resistance to convince you to back up. Something on the inside of you has to stand up and say, "In spite of resistance and

rejection, I am going to break through—it does not matter what anyone else says or thinks about it. I will break through."

Many people live their lives expecting to be rejected, looking for someone to disagree with them, disapprove of them, or not accept them. Secretly, they hope that someone will do so and give them an excuse to give up on their dream. We, as leaders, coaches, and trainers cannot afford to live like this. More than *our* futures are at stake. Instead, we must learn to live as though there were a "yes" over our lives, like there is a promise of breakthrough over us. We must never forget that *the promises of God are yes and amen in Him* (2 Corinthians 1:20).

When you live with the belief that there is a "yes" over your life, it changes your whole mentality and outlook. It causes you to wake up looking for opportunities to take, beneficial relationships to cultivate, doors to open, and access to gain. You must believe that you are already approved, accepted, and valued by God. Remember that as Zerah made a way for Perez, Christ has already made a way for you.

Sometimes, when you are moving forward, when you are trying to break through, when you are trying to see something new birthed in your life, you will get a no. No, you cannot. No, you are not the one. Sometimes, when people hear the little two-letter word "no," everything in them falls apart. They had so much faith, strength, and courage . . . until somebody told them no. As if man's no is any

match for God's yes! If God has said, "Yes!" over your life, it does not matter who has told you no. He has already approved and given you the thumbs up. If I may—if God gives you the thumbs up, it does not matter what finger anyone else shows you!

This does not mean that you disregard others. It means that you recognize that God's yes overrides all others. So many people walk through life with a no—looking to be turned down, expecting things not to go their way, and anticipating their way to be blocked. They live their lives not looking, not expecting, and not anticipating something significant to happen in their favor. They forget that "if God is for us, who can be against us?" (Romans 8:31, NIV). When you are in Him, there is a promise, a yes, over your life.

Remember when Caleb and Joshua went to spy out the Promised Land? Notice the land had a name: Promised. God had already said, "Yes, it is yours." They went in, and they saw opportunity— big grapes and a land flowing with milk and honey. These were things they were going to enjoy. But the other spies—what did they see: giants, obstacles, and barriers. They could not see beyond the opposition to see the opportunity. Behind all opposition is an opportunity for God to do something remarkable, so He can demonstrate just how great a God He is.

As in the story of the Israelites and their Promised Land, God may allow the opposition to stay in your promised land for a while

because He knows it is going to produce some necessary things in you, like the character that will keep you in victory. This is why premature victory can be fatal. God had already promised the land to the children of Israel, but when they came to it, He did not tell all the giants to leave—He left the opposition right there in the land. You would think that if He had promised, He would have removed all the enemies out of their way. The fact that He left them there meant that He knew that the Israelites had more than what it took to drive them out. God allowing you and the people who look to you for guidance to encounter opposition proves that He believes that what He has put in you is greater than the opposition. "For whatever is born of God overcomes the world: and this is the victory that overcomes the world, even our faith. Who is he that overcomes the world, but he that believes that Jesus is the son of God?" (1 John 5:4-5, KJV). You are more than equipped to overcome any obstacle in front of you. Otherwise, He would have removed it already!

Sometimes, we see the opposition and we lose faith. We start to think that it is impossible, that it cannot happen, or that it was not meant to be. The opposition you face is proportional to your faith, ability, gifting, and grace. As the scripture says, "No temptation has seized you except what is common to man. And God is faithful; he will not let you be tempted beyond what you can bear. But, when you are tempted, he will also provide a way out so that you can stand up under it" (1 Corinthians 10:13, NIV). Opposition can be

evidence that an opportunity is waiting for you. Why else would the enemy waste his time fighting you?

When people meet opposition, they often believe that God is punitive, that He is out to get them, and that He is somehow displeased or dissatisfied with them. They think He is trying to settle a score because of something they did. God is not like that. He is not looking for a reason to get you. If He wanted to get you, He would have already gotten you!

The God we serve is full of love, forgiveness, grace, mercy, acceptance, and approval, and the people we lead need to hear that now more than ever. He is already for us, even more than we are for ourselves! That is why the old folks used to say, "He's been better to me than I've been to myself!" He has a lot of confidence in what He has put in you, which is a bit of Himself. As the scripture teaches, "So, God created man in his own image, in the image of God He created him; male and female He created them" (Genesis 1:27, NIV).

You, therefore, must believe that you can win, you can do it, you can have it, and you can make it happen. You can see your dream become a reality. You can see that vision manifest. You can be successful. You can be prosperous. God wants you to succeed even more than you want to succeed, and He wants that confidence to be instilled in those who look to you for guidance.

PRACTICAL POINTS: BREAKING THE FEAR OF OPPOSITION

When life kicks you, make it kick you forward. In life, adversity is inevitable. In any significant pursuit, there will be opposition. No one is exempt from it. Adversity comes to expose who you are on the inside. Ordinary people, many times, become bitter when faced with adversity. Breakthrough people, however, become better. To break the fear of opposition, they create a strategy to overcome it before it even arrives. That strategy entails the following:

FACE IT.

Knowing that opposition is guaranteed, determine to face it head-on. When opposition tries to stare us down and cause us to back up and quit, we must reach down and remember that the greater One lives inside of us. Purpose to look adversity straight in the face. Do not walk in denial or stick your head in the sand. It is what it is. Understand that most adversity does not disappear with just the passage of time—you have to deal with the struggle or challenge. The sooner you do, the sooner you can turn the setback into a comeback. The power of confrontation strengthens you to hold your ground and not lose what belongs to you. Only when you are willing to confront are you in a position to conquer.

LEARN FROM IT.

Breakthrough people understand that adversity can be a great teacher. Not only does it teach us what to do, it also teaches us what not to do. Sometimes the greatest teachers in life will be our enemies. Some lessons we will never learn if we do not have enemies. Through overcoming our enemies, we learn more about ourselves, others, and God. When opposition comes, begin to ask strategic questions that will give you the insight needed to gain the victory. In order to get better—and not bitter—we must purpose to learn the lessons that are essential for success while we are facing opposition.

ASK FOR HELP.

When we begin to ask those strategic questions, it is important to remember that we cannot ask everybody! We must have the right people on our teams, and we must be the right people on other people's teams. Then, we can ask them for their wisdom and insight from their experiences. When adversity comes, that is not the time to get caught up in arrogance. Never be too proud to ask for help. Never fall into the trap of thinking that you have to know it all. Breakthrough people understand that they do not have to know all the answers, but they have to know where to look for answers and how to identify them when they see them.

KEEP THINGS IN PERSPECTIVE.

When most of the spies we mentioned earlier saw the Promised Land, they saw themselves as grasshoppers. They were looking at themselves from the perspective of the opposition. Breakthrough people have a winner's perspective. That is, they see themselves as God sees them—possessors of the Promised Land! They do not permit the opposition to define them. They size up the opposition relative to God, who is greater. To break through, you must keep the opposition in perspective. It is not personal—it rains on the just and the unjust (see Matthew 5:45). It is not invincible—you can overcome it. It is not permanent—this, too, shall pass. Even better, there is no opposition anywhere in creation that is bigger than God. He rules over everything, and because of that, we can win.

QUESTIONS FOR REFLECTION

ASK YOURSELF OR THOSE YOU LEAD, MENTOR OR COUNSEL:

- How does opposition manifest in your life?

- Can you think of a specific time when resistance forced you to give up on your dream?

- Since God is a God of second chances, ask Him for the courage to face your opposition and move forward in

spite of the giants in your land. From your past experience, how will you deal with it the next time you see it? Write down your action plan for facing opposition.

▪ What challenges do you need to face head-on?

▪ What lessons have you learned from dealing with resistance?

▪ Who are the people on your team who can help you overcome opposition?

▪ How does your perspective need to change in regards to opposition?

CHAPTER 7

SUSTAINING BREAKTHROUGH

He who is not every day conquering some
fear has not learned the secret of life.
—Ralph Waldo Emerson[31]

As we come to the end of *Breakthrough Is in You*, I would like to remind you that limitless possibilities are within you. There are dreams to be realized. The capacity to break through barriers and overcome obstacles is waiting to be awakened. But to live your dream and experience those possibilities and guide others to do the same, you must be willing to stare your fears in the face every day. You must purpose in your heart to face those fears that threaten to paralyze you in your current position. There must be a resolve to refuse to be conquered by FEAR—false evidence appearing real.

31 Ralph Waldo Emerson Quotes. BrainyQuote.com, BrainyMedia Inc, 2021. https://www.brainyquote.com/quotes/ralph_waldo_emerson_121501, accessed April 15, 2021.

I have identified five fears that must be broken in order for you to break through into another level of success, achievement, and fulfillment:

1) The Fear of the Unknown
2) The Fear of Failure
3) The Fear of Being First
4) The Fear of Investment
5) The Fear of Opposition

Any time one of these fears surfaces, face it immediately. Do not let it take root in your mind and heart. If you allow them, they will paralyze you and abort your breakthrough. You must endeavor to sustain your breakthrough.

Barbara Garrison once said, "Fear grows out of the things we think; it lives in our minds. Compassion grows out of the things we are and lives in our hearts."[32] Overcoming fear begins with a shift in our thinking. The thoughts that fill our minds either propel us into our future or paralyze us in our present. Thoughts are extremely powerful. A person always moves in the direction of his or her dominant thoughts.

---

32 "'Fear Grows out of the Things We Think; It Lives in Our Minds. Compassion Grows out of the Things We Are, and Lives in Our Hearts.'." passiton.com. Accessed April 15, 2021. https://www.passiton.com/inspirational-quotes/7233-fear-grows-out-of-the-things-we-think-it-lives.

If we believe we can accomplish something, we will find a way to make it happen. Neil Armstrong demonstrated this when he overcame the fear of the unknown and walked on the moon. Steve Jobs showed how to break the fear of failure when he persevered until he accomplished some of the greatest technological advances of our generation. James Meredith modeled courage when he broke through and became the first African American admitted to attend the University of Mississippi. Mother Teresa modeled how to remove the fear of investment when she gave her life to help those whom the world had forgotten. Nelson Mandela exemplified the tenacity to overcome the fear of opposition and defeated apartheid. Thirteen-year-old Jordan Romero joined their ranks when he became the youngest climber to reach the top of Mt. Everest. They broke through. Each of these people was driven by thoughts that caused him or her to reach for dreams instead of settling for the status quo.

Garrison's quote speaks of not only the thoughts of the mind, but also the passion that lives in the heart. In reading this book, I hope the passion of your heart has been stirred, and that you have found the drive to maximize your moment and seize your opportunities. My hope is that the real you will begin to stand up and wholeheartedly live out a passionate pursuit of purpose that will be an example to others of what it means to be a breakthrough person.

My prayer for you is that you will aspire for more and that the dynamic, power, and capacity to break through will come alive

in your life. I pray that every fear would be broken—especially the Fear of the Unknown, the Fear of Failure, the Fear of Going First, the Fear of Investment, and the Fear of Opposition. I pray that faith, boldness and confidence would arise in your heart and cause you to go forward, knowing that if you do not quit, you will succeed. If you do not give up, you will win, because breakthrough is in you.

ABOUT THE AUTHOR

Jeff Scott Smith is the Lead Pastor of Strong Tower Church in Fredericksburg, Virginia. Strong Tower is a thriving congregation located just south of Washington, DC.

It is a place of restoration and hope for people from all walks of life. Today it continues to make a significant impact throughout the central Virginia region and around the world.

Pastor Smith's communication style is passionate, practical, and engaging. His focus is on reaching people with the empowering message of Jesus Christ, developing leaders and building the local church.

Pastor Smith received a Bachelor of Science Degree in Finance from Bowling Green State University and a Masters in Organizational Leadership from Regent University. Pastor Smith has a passion for helping pastors and leaders push their vision forward. As president of JSS Consulting Inc., he helps today's leaders reach new heights in ministry. He is also a certified executive coach

through the world-renowned Hudson Institute of Coaching in Santa Barbara, California. His extensive corporate and ministry background has made him uniquely qualified to assist pastors and leaders in reaching their next level. After years of working with pastors and leaders, he has developed keen insight in the areas of strategic planning, leadership development, systems implementation, and enhancing staff productivity. He is sought after internationally for his expertise in consulting leaders and helping them realize their untapped potential. In addition, Pastor Smith serves as Director of Cornerstone Global Network under the leadership of Bishop Michael Pitts. It is a network of over 80 churches throughout the United States, Mexico, and the U.K.

FAVORITE QUOTES

Fear is only as deep as the mind allows.
—Japanese Proverb

If you are distressed by anything external,
the pain is not due to the thing itself,
but to your estimate of it:
and this you have the power to revoke at any moment.
—Marcus Aurelius

The enemy is fear. We think it is hate: but, it is fear.
—Gandhi

Curiosity will conquer fear even more than bravery will.
—James Stephens

I must not fear.
Fear is the mind-killer.
Fear is the little-death that brings total obliteration.
I will face my fear.
I will permit it to pass over me and through me.
And when it has gone past I will turn
the inner eye to see its path.
Where the fear has gone there will be nothing.
Only I will remain.
—Frank Herbert

You gain strength, courage, and confidence by every
experience in which you really stop to look fear in the face.
You must do the thing which you think you cannot do.
—Eleanor Roosevelt

Inaction breeds doubt and fear. Action
breeds confidence and courage.
If you want to conquer fear, do not sit home and think about it.
Go out and get busy.
—Dale Carnegie

God has not given us a spirit of fear but of
love, power and a sound mind.
—2 Timothy 1:7